Contents

Words in **bold** are explained in the glossary on page 30.

A healthy boy

It was a bright April day in Stratford-upon-Avon, Warwickshire, in the year 1564. The sun was shining down on the busy little town, and people were hurrying to the market to do their shopping.

In a big house in Henley Street, Mary Shakespeare lay in bed, sweating and groaning. She was about to have her third baby. But Mary was worried.

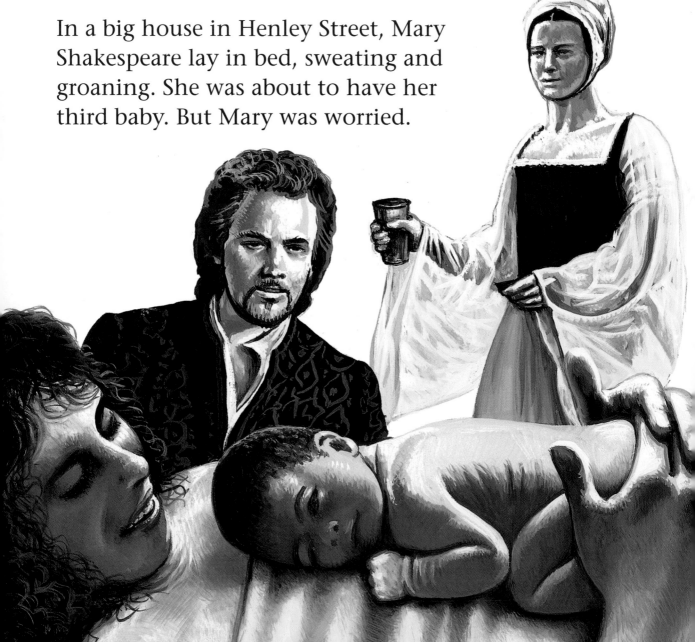

The house in Stratford-upon-Avon where William Shakespeare was born.

Many babies did not survive in those days and her first two babies had died. A wave of pain gripped her. She let out a roar, gave a big push and the baby was born. It was a little boy. Mary and her husband, John, decided to call their son William. They prayed that this child would live.

That year, the **plague** swept through England. The deadly disease, carried by rats' fleas, killed 200 people in Stratford. Luckily for the Shakespeares, little William survived.

Young Will

William soon had two brothers and two sisters, Gilbert, Richard, Joan and Anne. His father, John Shakespeare, was a glove maker and his mother had **inherited** some farmland and money. So his family was quite well off.

William's father worked at home making fine leather gloves. He sold them on his stall under the clock-tower in Stratford marketplace. His business was successful and the townspeople admired him.

When William was four, the townspeople made his father High Bailiff of Stratford. This was a bit like being the mayor and it made William's father very important in the town. He wore a red robe with fur on it when he went to the town's big **events**.

One of William's father's jobs was to give **licences** to actors who were visiting the town. These allowed the actors to put on their plays and the Shakespeares went to see the performances. William was thrilled by the excitement of the plays.

William and his father watch a play put on in the open air. ▼

7

School-days

Only boys went to school in Shakespeare's time. William's first school was Petty School, where he learned to read and write. Around the age of seven, he went to the grammar school in Stratford. There he learned Latin and studied the Bible and history. In the top classes, no one was allowed to speak English. They had to speak in Latin, which is the old language of the Romans.

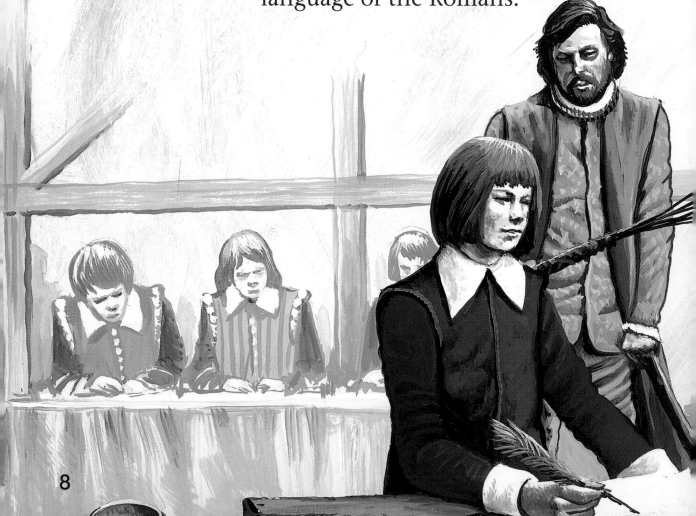

▲ The top floor of this building was the grammar school where William was a pupil.

The school day was very long and tiring. William started school at 6 am and didn't finish until 5 pm. He had to go to school six days a week and did not get many holidays. When the boys were naughty, they were hit with a **birch-rod**. One boy carved this complaint in Latin on a desk: 'Nothing comes from working hard.'

▲ The grammar school had just this one classroom.

When William was twelve, his father suddenly had money problems. So William had to leave school to help his father with the glove business.

Marriage and children

When William was eighteen, he met Anne Hathaway, the daughter of a farmer. Anne lived about a kilometre away from William, across the fields in the village of Shottery. She was twenty-six years old. Anne and William were married in November 1582.

Anne moved into William's parents' house in Stratford. In May 1583, she gave birth to their first child, Susanna. Two years later Anne had twins, a boy called Hamnet and a girl called Judith. By the age of twenty-one, William was the father of three children.

▲ Anne Hathaway's cottage.

10

Shortly after the twins were born, William left Stratford. His wife and children stayed behind. No one knows why William left or where he went. Some say he went to work for a **lawyer**. Others think he became a teacher. One story says he was caught poaching Sir Thomas Lucy's deer from Charlecote Park near Stratford and had to run away to London.

William leaves Anne and the twins in Stratford. ▼

London and the theatre

Sometime between 1585 and 1592, William arrived at the gates of the city of London. He looked around in amazement. Huge ships were sailing up the River Thames into the heart of the walled city. Up above him, **traitors'** heads were stuck on poles on London Bridge Gate. Horses' hooves clattered through the narrow streets, and laughter spilled from the busy inns.

William decided to stay. He found himself **lodgings** and set out to look for work.

▲ London in Shakespeare's time, with London Bridge in the centre of the picture. You can see the traitors' heads over the gate at this end of the bridge.

12

William soon decided to work in the theatre. There were lots of jobs to do – sweeping the floor, reminding the actors when to go on stage, and looking after people's horses while they watched the plays.

Going to the theatre was very different from today. It was a bit like going to a football match. Plays were only put on in the daytime. People started to queue early in the day. It cost one penny to stand round the stage, and twopence for a seat and a roof over your head. Rich people paid to sit on balconies.

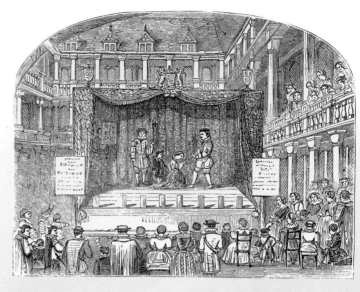

▲ A theatre company puts on a play in an inn yard.

14

While the **audience** waited for the play to start, they chatted to their friends. They bought **ale** and nibbled nuts and apples. Sometimes a **cutpurse** would sneak through the crowd stealing purses. If he was caught, he was tied up on stage during the **interval** and the crowd threw apple cores at him.

Outside the theatre a woman sells apples and a cutpurse tries to steal money. ▼

William loved watching the plays. There were tales from the Bible, battles from history, love stories and **comedies**.

The stage was huge, and the audience was very close to the actors. The actors came on to the stage through a door at the back and wore beautiful costumes.

▲ A theatre in Shakespeare's time. People paid more to sit on the balconies.

Drums rolled, trumpets called, lightning flashed and cannon roared. Some actors hid **bladders** full of pigs' blood and animal guts under their shirts. When they were 'stabbed' during the play, the bladders burst and spilt blood and guts all over the stage.

It was so exciting that William decided to become an actor and to write his own plays. He was enjoying life in London, but he missed his family. So once a year he went home to Stratford to visit them.

William reminds actors of their words. ▶

16

A successful playwright

The plays William wrote were very popular. Huge crowds queued to see the bloodthirsty play *Titus Andronicus*. In this play, Titus's daughter is attacked by some men who are brothers. Titus catches the brothers, cuts them up and puts them in a pie. Then he feeds the pie to their mother!

Shakespeare's play *Henry VI* was such a success that it was put on fifteen times at the Rose Theatre in one year.

A scene from *Henry VI.* ▼

William (sitting in the centre) and some other famous men of his time. Sitting behind William is his friend Ben Jonson, who was also a playwright.

Most of the other successful **playwrights** in London, like Christopher Marlowe, had been to **university**. William had not, and many people looked down on him because of this. But it did not stop him from becoming successful.

The plague

Carts full of dead to bury.

◀ In 1592, the plague swept through London's overcrowded slums, killing 10,000 people.

In 1592 the plague struck London. The theatres were closed to stop the disease spreading through the audience crowds. While they were shut, William wrote a poem called *The Rape of Lucrece* for the Earl of Southampton. Some people say the young earl paid William £1,000 for the poem.

Then William wrote 154 beautiful poems called sonnets. He wrote the sonnets for his friends, but soon everyone wanted to read them.

In 1594 the theatres opened again. William gave up writing poetry and went back to his plays. He worked very hard, writing two or three plays a year and acting in many more.

▼ The Earl of Southampton.

While the theatres were closed, Christopher Marlowe had been stabbed in a fight in a London inn. William's greatest **rival** was dead.

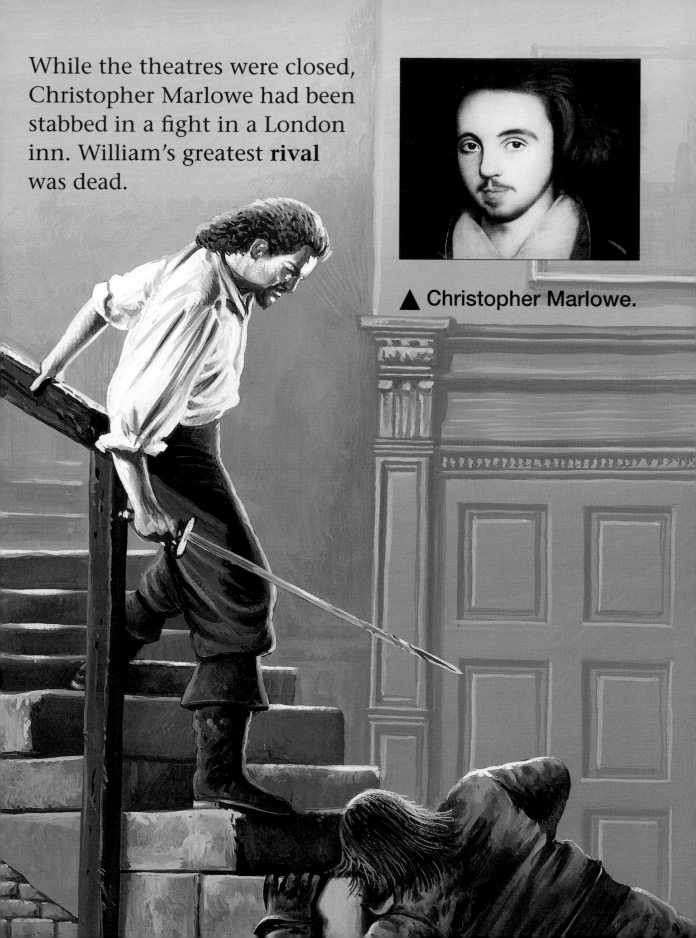

▲ Christopher Marlowe.

William got the ideas for his plays from old stories, poems and real events. His plays made audiences laugh, and cry, and gasp in horror.

A Midsummer Night's Dream is a very funny play. William probably wrote it for a wedding that Queen Elizabeth I went to. In this play, a naughty fairy puts a magic love potion on Queen Titania's eyes while she is asleep. The potion will make her fall in love with the first person she sees when she wakes up. The first person Titania sees is a poor weaver called Bottom. He looks very silly because he is wearing a donkey's head.

▲ Scenes from *A Midsummer Night's Dream.* ▼

William's play *Romeo and Juliet* is one of the most famous love stories in the world. Romeo and Juliet fall in love, but their families hate each other and will not let them marry. So the young lovers plan to run away. But the plan goes wrong and the couple end up killing themselves.

A royal favourite

The Globe
Theatre. ▶

Queen Elizabeth I
loved watching
Shakespeare's
plays. ▼

William carried on acting as well as writing. He belonged to a group of actors called the Lord Chamberlain's Men. They often acted at Queen Elizabeth's **court**. The queen liked Falstaff in William's play *Henry IV*. So he wrote another play about Falstaff, *The Merry Wives of Windsor,* specially for her.

By the time William was thirty-three, he was making a lot of money and was famous. He bought New Place, the second-biggest house in Stratford, and went there often to visit his family. Gradually he bought more and more land. Then he bought a share in London's finest theatre, the Globe. It was on the south bank of the River Thames and was made of wood.

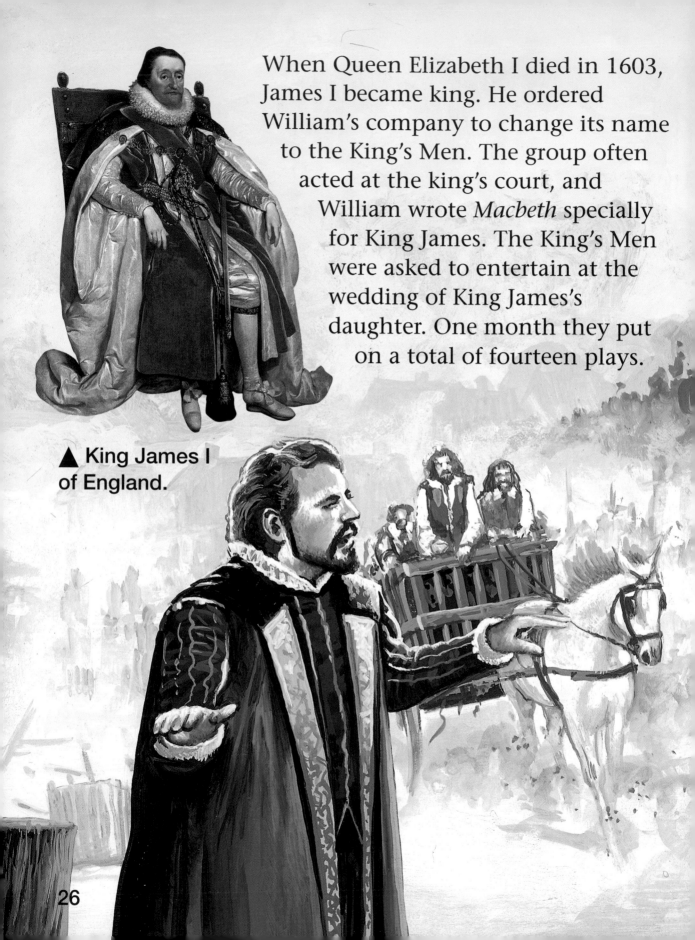

When Queen Elizabeth I died in 1603, James I became king. He ordered William's company to change its name to the King's Men. The group often acted at the king's court, and William wrote *Macbeth* specially for King James. The King's Men were asked to entertain at the wedding of King James's daughter. One month they put on a total of fourteen plays.

▲ King James I of England.

In June 1613, William's play *Henry VIII* was put on at the Globe Theatre. During the play, a cannon shot out a burning paper ball. It landed on the thatched roof of the theatre. Soon the whole building was on fire. Within an hour it was burnt to the ground.

The final years

After the fire at the Globe Theatre in 1613, Shakespeare decided to **retire** from work and return to Stratford to be with his family. He was forty-nine years old and had written thirty-seven plays. His daughters, Susanna and Judith, had both grown up and married, but his son, Hamnet, had died.

▲ New Place, in Stratford.

In 1616 William wrote his will. He left most of his land and property to his family. He also left money to the poor people of Stratford. But his greatest treasure, his writing, was left for the whole world to enjoy.

William died on 23 April 1616 at the age of fifty-two. He was buried two days later in Holy Trinity Church. On his gravestone is a warning that he might have written himself:

*'Blessed be the man that
   spares these stones
And cursed be he that
   moves my bones.'*

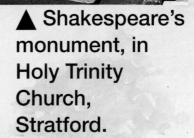

▲ Shakespeare's monument, in Holy Trinity Church, Stratford.

Glossary

ale Beer.

audience A group of people who watch a play.

birch-rod A bundle of twigs or a stick from a birch tree, used to hit someone.

bladders Thin bags of skin or other material that are easily stretched by the liquid or air inside them.

comedies Funny plays.

court A king or queen's home and their attendants.

cutpurse An old word for a pickpocket or thief. People did not have pockets in Shakespeare's time. Thieves stole money from people by taking their purses.

events Important things that happen, such as plays or concerts.

inherited Passed down by a relative who has died.

interval A break in the middle of a play.

lawyer A person who is an expert in the law.

licences Pieces of paper giving permission for something.

lodgings A rented room in another person's house.

plague A deadly disease, caught from the bites of rats' fleas, which spreads quickly through crowds.

playwrights People who write plays.

retire To give up a regular job or profession.

rival A person who is in competition with another person.

traitors People who have helped their country's enemy.

university A place for higher education after school.

Date chart

1564 Shakespeare is born in Stratford-upon-Avon.
1582 Marries Anne Hathaway.
1583 Daughter Susanna is born.
1585 Twins, Hamnet and Judith, are born.
1585–92 Shakespeare moves to London.
1592 The plague. Theatres close in London.
1593 Christopher Marlowe dies.

1594 Theatres open again.
1597 Shakespeare buys New Place, in Stratford.
1603 Queen Elizabeth I dies. James I becomes King of England.
Lord Chamberlain's Men change their name to the King's Men.
1613 The Globe Theatre burns down. Shakespeare retires to Stratford.
1616 Shakespeare dies.

Books to read

Great Lives: William Shakespeare by Dorothy Turner (Wayland, 1985)
Shakespeare, the Animated Tales: Twelfth Night abridged by Leon Garfield (Heinemann, 1992)
Shakespeare for Everyone: Hamlet by Jennifer Mulherin (Cherrytree Press, 1988)
Shakespeare for Everyone: Macbeth by Jennifer Mulherin (Cherrytree Press, 1988)
Shakespeare for Everyone: Romeo and Juliet by Jennifer Mulherin (Cherrytree Press, 1988)

Index

The publishers would like to thank the following for allowing their photographs to be used in this book: Ben Christopher/Performing Arts Library 22; Mary Evans *Cover*, Title page, 14; Michael Holford 12; Hulton Deutsch 19, 20 (bottom), 21; Jarrold Publishing 9, 10, 28, 29; National Portrait Gallery 26; Topham 5, 8, 20; Wayland Picture Library 16, 24.

Contents

INTRODUCTION

When William Shakespeare wrote *Twelfth Night*, probably in 1601, he was enjoying huge success as an actor and playwright in the theatre in London. He was one of the leaders of the company of actors to which he belonged, The Lord Chamberlain's Men, and his plays were drawing large audiences to The Globe, their new theatre on the south bank of the Thames.

All companies of actors needed the support and protection of powerful noblemen to prevent them from being arrested as vagabonds (homeless beggars). Shakespeare and his fellow actors had an important patron in the Lord Chamberlain. He was one of Queen Elizabeth I's ministers and his duties included organizing the entertainments for the Queen and her guests. The Lord Chamberlain's Men were required to perform at court several times a year.

This earned them good money and immense prestige. Shakespeare, who as a young man had come to London from the small market town of Stratford-upon-Avon in Warwickshire, had made his mark.

FEASTING AND FOOLING

The full title of the play – *Twelfth Night, Or What You Will* – suggests something lighthearted. The twelfth and last day of Christmas, 6 January, was celebrated riotously. The day of feasting and fooling was often led by a 'Lord of Misrule', someone chosen to create disorder, and dramatic entertainment, music and dancing were all part of the fun.

The Lord Chamberlain's Men performed at court on Twelfth Night 1601 as part of the Queen's lavish Christmas celebrations. It is just possible that the play they presented was *Twelfth Night*. More likely, Shakespeare wrote his play after that event, perhaps partly inspired by it.

The Hall of the Middle Temple, one of the Inns of Court in London, where *Twelfth Night* was performed on 2 February 1602.

AN EARLY PERFORMANCE

It is known that *Twelfth Night* was performed in the Hall of the Middle Temple in London on 2 February 1602 and this may have been its first performance. The Middle Temple was one of the Inns of Court, where young men training to be lawyers lived and studied. One of them, John Massingham, wrote an account of the performance in his diary:

'... at our feast we had a play called Twelfth Night Or What You Will. *A good practice to make the steward believe his lady was in love with him ...'*

SOURCES

Shakespeare was never shy about using other people's work as the basis for his plays. For *Twelfth Night* he used much of the story of a romantic tale called *Farewell to Militarie Profession* published by Barnaby Riche in 1581. This was itself based on an Italian play, *Gl'Ingannati* ('The Deceptions'), performed in 1531. What is interesting are the additions Shakespeare made to these originals. He sets his play in Illyria – now Croatia – although he turns it into an imaginary country, at once strange, and yet with many features of his own London. For his play, Shakespeare added four new characters: **Sir Toby Belch**, **Sir Andrew Aguecheek**, **Malvolio** and **Feste**. They not only add much to the comedy of the play, they also extend the range of its moods.

Twelfth Night is a very funny play, but it has elements of seriousness which constantly remind the audience that young people grow old and die, that though we may laugh, tears are never far away, and that the search for love can be tender, or painful, or even downright foolish.

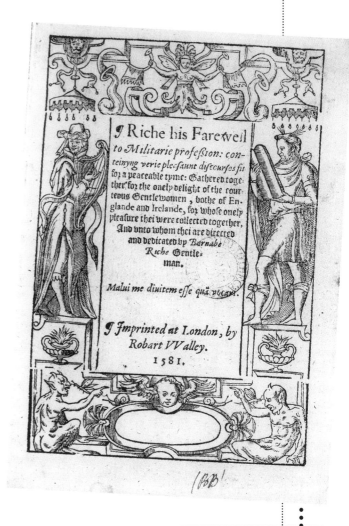

The frontispiece to Barnaby Riche's romantic tale, *Farewell to Militarie Profession*, a source for much of the plot of *Twelfth Night*.

THE CHARACTERS

Orsino is the Duke of Illyria. He is courting Olivia, a countess.

Valentine and **Curio** are courtiers – gentlemen who attend Orsino.

Viola is a young lady who lands on Illyria when her ship is wrecked in a storm at sea. She disguises herself as a boy, **Cesario**, and serves Orsino.

There is a **Sea Captain** who helps Viola.

Sebastian is Viola's twin brother.

Antonio is another sea captain and a friend of Sebastian.

Olivia is a countess, living in Illyria.

Maria is Olivia's gentlewoman, her servant and companion.

Sir Toby Belch is Olivia's uncle, living in her household.

Sir Andrew Aguecheek is a companion of Sir Toby. He has come to Olivia's house in the hope that she will agree to marry him.

Malvolio is Olivia's steward. He is her chief servant with responsibility for her household.

Fabian is another servant in Olivia's household.

Feste is Olivia's fool or jester – her household entertainer.

There is also a **Priest** and other **servants**, **officers**, **musicians** and **sailors**.

'With hey, ho, the wind and the rain.'
An early twentieth century drawing of Feste by W. Heath Robinson.

Freddie Jones as Malvolio
at the Royal Shakespeare
Company (RSC), 1991.

WHAT HAPPENS
IN THE PLAY

Orsino is in love, but **Olivia**, the woman he loves, will have nothing to do with him. **Curio**, a gentleman in Orsino's court, tries in vain to get the duke to think of other things. Then **Valentine**, another of the duke's attendants, comes with a message from Olivia. She is still rejecting Orsino; she is in mourning for her brother who has died and refuses to think of anything else.

Meanwhile, a storm off the coast of Illyria has wrecked a ship carrying **Viola**, a young woman, and her twin brother **Sebastian**. Viola has been saved by a **Sea Captain** but they fear that Sebastian has been drowned.

The captain tells Viola where they are, and about the situation between Orsino and Olivia. Viola has heard of Orsino before from her father. Alone now, and in a strange country, she decides the best thing will be to dress as a young man and try to get employment at Orsino's court:

'What else may hap [happen] to time I will commit.'

'What country, friends, is this?' Cherie Lunghi as Viola and the Sea Captain from the RSC's 1979 production.

At Olivia's house **Sir Toby Belch**, her hard-drinking uncle, is being given a warning by **Maria**, the countess's lady-in-waiting. She has heard Olivia making unfavourable comments about Sir Toby's bad habits, and about **Sir Andrew Aguecheek**, whom Sir Toby has brought into the household. If they don't behave themselves, Olivia is likely to throw them out.

A BATTLE OF WITS

Sir Toby protests that Sir Andrew is brave, clever and rich. Maria thinks he's a fool. Sir Andrew comes in, and it's clear at once that Maria is right: she runs rings round him in a battle of wits. When she has left them, Sir Toby tells Sir Andrew that he needs a drink to improve his wits. But Aguecheek is fed up: Olivia wants nothing to do with him; he might as well go home. However, the promise of a good time drinking and dancing makes him quickly change his mind.

VIOLA BECOMES CESARIO

Viola has dressed herself as a boy and become an attendant at Orsino's court, calling herself **Cesario**. Orsino is so taken with the new arrival that he decides to send Cesario to Olivia in the hope that this new messenger will make the countess change her mind. Viola agrees to go but with some doubts: she is already falling in love with Orsino herself:

> *'Whoe'er I woo, myself would be his wife.'*

FESTE AND MALVOLIO

At Olivia's house, **Feste**, her fool, has been missing. Now he has turned up, Maria tells him he's in trouble. But his wit turns Maria's anger into sympathy as Olivia and **Malvolio** arrive. Olivia is still angry with Feste and tells him to go away, but Feste boldly turns this on her, calling her a fool. She is annoyed but fascinated – what does Feste mean? He asks for permission to show her. He asks why she is in mourning. 'For my brother's death,' she replies. He must be in hell, says Feste. Olivia retorts that he's in heaven. 'The more fool … to mourn for your brother's soul, being in heaven.' So Feste has both comforted and amused Olivia.

Malvolio is not so easily appeased – he doesn't like Feste's wit. Olivia accuses him of being 'sick of self-love' (so pompous and sure of himself that he can't enjoy humour) and praises Feste. As an 'allowed fool' it's his job to speak the truth and to make fun, however hard that might be to accept; it can only be for the good in the end.

Maria announces another messenger, arrived from Orsino. Olivia tells Malvolio to send him away and he's hardly gone before Sir Toby arrives. Although it's still morning, he's very drunk. He too has come to tell Olivia that 'a gentleman' is at the gate. Sir Toby wanders away, followed by Maria.

OLIVIA AND CESARIO

All Malvolio's efforts to send the messenger away have failed:

'He'll speak with you, will you or no.'

Malvolio describes the young man – he's obviously handsome and Olivia wants to know more. She calls for Maria and sends Malvolio off to fetch Orsino's man. Olivia and Maria decide to play a trick on the youth. They both put veils over their faces and when Cesario comes in he has to ask which is Olivia. At first they won't tell him, but he refuses to give his message to anyone but Olivia. Olivia tells Cesario he must leave.

Maria tries to take him away, but Cesario refuses to go, insisting on giving his message from the duke. Olivia relents – Cesario is, after all, a handsome young man. Maria is sent away and Cesario begins. He soon stops, though, and asks to see Olivia's face. She lifts her veil, proud of her beauty. 'Is't not well done?' she asks, meaning 'Am I not beautiful?' Viola is taken aback. Olivia is indeed beautiful, and she is Viola's rival for Orsino. So Viola, in her disguise as Cesario, answers wittily and cuttingly:

'Excellently done, if God did all.'

In other words, 'You certainly seem to be beautiful, but how much of that is your make-up!'

Antonio shows himself a true friend to Sebastian. Stratford, 1993.

Viola/Cesario delivers the message from Orsino and Olivia is hooked – not by the message but by the messenger. She asks Cesario to come back again when she will give an answer to the duke. Cesario goes. Now the countess calls for Malvolio and hands him a ring. She says it is from Orsino, and must be returned to Cesario; in fact, she's giving it to Cesario as a gift – Olivia has fallen in love.

SEBASTIAN

Back at the coast, another young person has been washed ashore after the shipwreck. Sebastian is mourning the loss of his twin sister, whom he believes to have been drowned in the wreck from which he has been saved. Sebastian is making for Orsino's court. His companion, **Antonio**, knows of the place. Although he is a wanted man there, following a recent war between his country and Orsino's, Antonio decides to follow Sebastian.

MALVOLIO, CESARIO AND THE RING

Meanwhile, Malvolio catches up with Cesario and tries to hand over the ring, which he believes to be a gift from Orsino which Olivia has rejected. Viola/Cesario is bewildered – she didn't give Olivia a ring from Orsino. However, she covers up for Olivia by saying that the countess actually took the ring off her. When Cesario refuses to take the ring, Malvolio drops it on the ground in front of Cesario and walks away.

Alone now, Viola/Cesario reflects on the situation. She is beginning to see the truth and to understand what Olivia is doing:

'She loves me ... Poor thing, she were better love a dream.'

Viola realizes that the game she is playing has become serious:

'My master loves her dearly;
And I, poor monster, fond as much on him;
And she, mistaken, seems to dote on me ...
O time, thou must untangle this, not I!
It is too hard a knot for me t'untie.''

CAKES AND ALE

It is late at night at Olivia's house. Sir Toby and Sir Andrew have been out drinking and come in, noisy and drunk. Sir Toby shouts for more wine. Feste comes to them and they persuade him to sing for them. Feste sings a sad love song: 'O Mistress Mine'. It seems to sadden them, and Belch shouts for a jollier song. All three of them are soon singing at the tops of their voices. They wake Maria who tries, completely unsuccessfully, to calm them down. They have also woken Malvolio, who attempts to bring them to order, but they mock him and refuse to be quiet. Sir Toby turns on Malvolio:

'Dost thou think, because thou art virtuous, there shall be no more cakes and ale?'

MARIA'S PLOT

Malvolio leaves, threatening to tell Olivia what's been going on. This is the last straw for the revellers and they start to work out a plot to make Malvolio look a fool. Maria says that her handwriting is like Olivia's and she will write a letter to trap Malvolio into an embarrassing situation. Maria may well see Malvolio as her rival in Olivia's household: she seems only too pleased to undermine his position! She goes off to bed while Sir Toby persuades Sir Andrew to join him in another drink.

ORSINO AND CESARIO

Viola/Cesario is back at Orsino's court. Feste is with them (although Olivia's fool, he performs anywhere if he's paid). He sings another sad love song: 'Come away, death'. Then Orsino tells Cesario he's more lovesick than any woman could be.

But Viola makes up a story about her 'sister' who pined away for love. Moved by this, Orsino asks if the girl died. Realizing how close she is to telling Orsino the truth about herself she answers him with a riddle:

'I am all the daughters of my father's house,
And all the brothers too; and yet I know not ...'

She quickly changes the subject and asks if she should go to Olivia again.

THE LETTER

Maria has written the letter, pretending it is from Olivia. She brings it to the garden where Belch, Aguecheek and another servant, **Fabian**, are waiting. She throws the letter down and they hide in a box-tree to see what will happen. Malvolio is out walking in the garden, day-dreaming about what life would be like if he were to be married to Olivia.

'My father had a daughter loved a man ...' The lovesick Orsino (Clive Wood) listens to Viola/Cesario (Emma Fielding), at Stratford in 1993.

He sees the letter, picks it up, opens it, and reads. He is sure it is from Olivia and is meant for him. The letter is a riddle which seems to be telling him that Olivia loves him and wants to promote him in his job as steward, and even to marry him.

'Some are born great, some achieve greatness, and some have greatness thrust upon 'em.'

The letter praises yellow stockings worn with garters and tells Malvolio to smile when he is with Olivia. Completely taken in, Malvolio goes off to find some yellow stockings and prepare to meet Olivia – smiling.

After he has gone the plotters celebrate the success of their trick. Maria points out that Olivia actually hates yellow stockings and garters, and if Malvolio smiles, it will only make her more angry.

RIVALS FOR OLIVIA

Cesario is on his way to Olivia's house when he meets Feste again. The fool begs money in exchange for witty remarks. When Feste has gone, Belch and Aguecheek arrive, soon followed by Olivia and Maria. Olivia tells the others to leave her alone with Cesario. When they have gone the countess again rejects Orsino.

But she tries to persuade his messenger to come back again. Cesario refuses and leaves.

Sir Andrew, too, has decided to leave: he's sure that Olivia loves Cesario. Toby persuades him that if that is the case, he'd better challenge the young man to a duel. Aguecheek leaves to write the letter of challenge as Maria arrives. She has seen Malvolio – dressed in yellow stockings and garters. He's on his way to Olivia with a smile on his face.

Meanwhile Sebastian and Antonio have arrived at the town near Orsino's court. Antonio explains that he is likely to be arrested if discovered. He asks Sebastian to look after his money and arranges to meet him at the place where they are staying later in the day.

Malvolio, played by Emrys James, reads Maria's mischievous letter in the RSC's 1983 production: 'Some are born great, some achieve greatness, and some have greatness thrust upon 'em.'

YELLOW STOCKINGS

At Olivia's house, Malvolio appears dressed in yellow stockings with fantastic cross-garters. Olivia is amazed and, when Malvolio seems unable to stop smiling at her, is convinced he has gone mad. She tells Maria, Fabian and Sir Toby to take care of Malvolio but, after she's gone, they just wind Malvolio up even more.

The steward leaves and Sir Andrew arrives with his letter for Cesario. It is a ridiculous challenge and Sir Toby decides to make still more trouble by delivering it in person. Olivia and Cesario approach and when Olivia has gone again, Sir Toby and Fabian tell Cesario that Sir Andrew wants to fight him. They make Aguecheek seem more fierce than he really is and when he returns they tell him that Cesario is a skilful fencer. Much against both their wills, they fight.

MISTAKEN IDENTITY

Almost at once Antonio appears. He mistakes Cesario for Sebastian and defends him. Then officers come to arrest Antonio, who asks Cesario for the money he has lent him. Viola/Cesario is completely mystified and Antonio thinks he has been betrayed by the man he thought was his friend. The officers take Antonio away, but Viola has heard the name of Sebastian – her twin brother!

A little while later Feste sees Sebastian. Thinking he is Cesario, he tells him Olivia has sent for him. Sebastian is confused but when Sir Toby and Sir Andrew appear to resume the quarrel, he draws his sword and beats them. Olivia arrives. She breaks up the fight and declares her love for the young man – thinking it is Cesario – and invites him into her house. Overwhelmed by her beauty, Sebastian follows her.

Malvolio has been locked away because of his 'madness'. Sir Toby and Maria persuade Feste to dress up as a clergyman – Sir Topas – and make fun of the steward. Protesting he is not mad, Malvolio asks for pen and paper to write to Olivia. Feste agrees: he is tired of the joke.

Sebastian comes out of Olivia's house in a lovesick daze. Olivia follows him with a priest. She asks Sebastian to marry her, still thinking he is Cesario. Sebastian agrees.

ALL IS REVEALED

Things move quickly to their climax. Feste arrives with the letter from Malvolio. Orsino and Cesario follow, and then Antonio with the officers. Antonio is trying to explain about Sebastian when Olivia arrives. Seeing Cesario, she calls him 'husband'. The priest confirms it. Orsino turns on Cesario for his falseness but is interrupted by Aguecheek who has been wounded – by the person he thinks is Cesario!

Again Cesario denies all knowledge of what's been going on. Then it happens – Sebastian joins them and the twins are united:

'One face, one voice, one habit and two persons!'

Feste now interrupts to remind them of Malvolio's letter. After she has read it, Olivia sends for the steward. While they are waiting, Orsino realizes he loves Viola, as Cesario has revealed 'himself' to be, and asks her to marry him. She agrees.

Malvolio arrives. The trick is explained but he will not forgive them. He stalks off threatening to get his own back: 'I'll be revenged on the whole pack of you!'

The loves are united: Sebastian and Olivia are married and so, we hear, are Sir Toby and Maria. Viola and Orsino will be married soon. Only Aguecheek is without a partner. But the play ends on a bitter-sweet note. No good thing lasts for ever, Feste sings at the close,

'For the rain it raineth every day.'

The company in the final scenes of the 1983 production at Stratford.

TWELFTH NIGHT...

At first sight the play looks like a great celebration. It is often funny, with lovely songs, and it seems to end happily with three couples about to embark on marriage. Yet, as so often in Shakespeare's works, the world of the play is much more complex, even disturbing, than first impressions might suggest.

This is a world where characters often doubt their sanity. 'Mad' and 'madness' are words which come up often in the play. They may be used in confused delight, as by **Sebastian**, 'Or am I mad, or else this is a dream.' Or they may be used cruelly, as by **Feste** when, as Sir Topas, he tells **Malvolio** that he is mad. Malvolio clings to his own sense of reality and insists: 'I am as well in my wits as any man in Illyria.'

UNRULY CELEBRATIONS

For the Elizabethans, Twelfth Night was a riotous feast, a blast of high spirits in the middle of winter. The celebration wasn't just eating and drinking. What was usually forbidden was encouraged by a 'Lord of Misrule', a sort of master of ceremonies, often a young boy, chosen to stir up the confusion. **Sir Toby Belch** and **Maria** are like a Lord and Lady of Misrule:

setting up the tricks to cut Malvolio down to size, encouraging the duel between **Sir Andrew** and **Cesario**, and generally encouraging noisy celebration and high jinks.

Even here, Shakespeare asks a darker and more serious question: Maria's letter, seeming to come from **Olivia**, does the trick and makes Malvolio look ridiculous. But then she, Sir Toby and Feste push it further, beyond the boundaries of fun and games. The Sir Topas episode is a cruel punishment of Malvolio, who stops being a figure of fun when he is locked up and left alone in the dark. Feste sees that the joke has got out of hand, and helps Malvolio write a letter to Olivia. Misrule has toppled into cruelty. All the fun and the fooling turn sour. Is Shakespeare asking the audience to consider how close humour can be to nastiness, how narrow the line is between being funny and being cruel?

THE VALUE OF TRUE FRIENDSHIP

Sir Toby's character is also worth questioning. On the surface he is the man who turns ordinary life into a party, who enjoys 'cakes and ale' and shares his own high spirits with everyone around him.

But is he simply a good man having a good time? What about his 'friendship' with Sir Andrew? Aguecheek's money is clearly one of his attractions: 'Send for money, knight.' It is questionable whether Sir Toby knows what being a true friend is about. He sets up the duel with Cesario and then brutally rejects Sir Andrew's affectionate offer of help by calling him insulting names when they have both been wounded by Sebastian.

What a contrast Sir Toby's changeable and often manipulative relationship with Sir Andrew is to that of Antonio with Sebastian. Antonio follows his friend into danger, saves him (so he thinks) in a duel, and is devastated when Cesario (who he thinks is Sebastian) rejects him.

Twelfth Night is a comedy that constantly exposes sadness and pain. This is clear in the character of Feste, the professional clown.

Turning up at Olivia's house at the beginning of the play after a long absence, he joins in the fun but always undercuts it with sad songs. At the end he is left alone to sing again – another hauntingly sad song about the hardness of life. Although Feste is a fool – an 'allowed fool', a professional teller of jokes and singer of songs – he is, in the end, wiser than all the rest, warning that life cannot always be easy and pleasurable.

'Pleasure will be paid one time or another ... The whirligig of time brings in his revenges.'

This painting by the Flemish artist Pieter Bruegel (c.1520–69) is of a peasant wedding. Twelfth Night celebrations would have been very similar.

... OR WHAT YOU WILL

Twelfth Night is a play about desire. It explores the confusions between what people think they want and what they really want. Love and friendship colour the play, but in wildly different moods. It opens with the lovesick **Orsino** moping about **Olivia**. His is a self-conscious obsession with no room for the rest of life. Orsino remains distant, sending messengers to plead for him whilst he acts the tormented lover at home. Since he never sees Olivia, he doesn't know if it is real love or not.

CONTRAST

This contrast between love of oneself and love of somebody else runs through the whole play. Self-love means thinking only about yourself and your feelings, while pretending to be concerned for others. True love means forgetting about yourself and being fully committed to the other person.

Olivia's fixation on the death of her brother suggests a similar personality to Orsino: her mourning is so inward-looking it has lost touch with reality, as **Feste** neatly and wittily shows her. **Viola**, on the other hand, believes her brother to be dead but doesn't turn her love or grief into a pose. She doesn't put on mourning clothes, she puts on boys' clothes.

She is realistic, deciding on a plan for her own survival. Yet her grief is real. She is desperate to remember every detail of the shipwreck, clinging to any faint hope that **Sebastian** might have survived: 'Perchance he is not drowned. What think you, sailors?'

DEEP FRIENDSHIP

Sebastian has not only survived, he has gained a remarkable friend and protector – **Antonio**. There are many deep, loving friendships in Shakespeare's plays and this is probably the most unselfish: a beautiful picture of one man's love for another, even though there is a risk of capture, torture and death. Antonio knows that he is a wanted man in Illyria, so it would be wise to leave as soon as possible. But love overcomes common sense.

Feste's wit jogs Olivia out of her tragic mood. Almost at once she forgets her sadness and her curiosity is aroused by the 'young man' at the gate. She lets Cesario deliver Orsino's latest love speeches and by the time she has heard them she is hopelessly in love with the messenger. But, 'poor lady, she were better love a dream.' Just as the Lord and Lady of Misrule seem to turn things on their head, so love is engaged in the same work.

Both Olivia and Orsino are in love with dreams: neither stops for long enough to ask what substance and reality there is to their feelings.

Aguecheek, too, is hopelessly pursuing Olivia, without ever facing the facts about the pointlessness of his courtship. **Malvolio** is so full of self-love that he allows himself to fantasize about marrying Olivia, and is trapped by **Maria**'s letter into thinking there's a chance that these dreams will come true. But eventually reality hits home: Orsino sees and responds to Viola's love; Olivia marries Sebastian (the male version of Cesario, as it were); Aguecheek leaves, a sadder, but probably no wiser, man. Malvolio stalks off, swearing revenge.

FINDING THE OTHER HALF

Above all, Viola and Sebastian find one another. Here Shakespeare is exploring a very old idea that everyone in the world is searching for their 'other half', which will make them 'whole'.

Viola and Sebastian, the twins, are the most telling example, but Viola and Orsino, Olivia and Sebastian, Sebastian and Antonio, even **Sir Toby** and Maria, show different ways in which two separate beings can come together as a single, loving whole. And so the confusions of *Twelfth Night* come to an end.

Nicholas Hilliard (1547–1619) was a fashionable painter of miniature portraits at the time of Shakespeare. He was court painter to Elizabeth I and James I. *A Youth Leaning Against A Tree Among Roses* shows us the kind of beautiful young man who might have been a courtier, as Viola/Cesario was to Orsino.

THE STAGE HISTORY OF
TWELFTH NIGHT

After the first recorded performance of *Twelfth Night* in 1602, it is almost certain that the play was regularly performed by the King's Men (as Shakespeare's company was renamed after King James I came to the throne in 1603). We know that when King Charles I saw it in 1623, it had been renamed *Malvolio*.

PURITANS

In **Malvolio**, Shakespeare draws a picture of a Puritan, obsessed with rules and regulations, full of his own importance, opposed to fun and games, but ambitious for power. Puritans believed that all men and women were responsible for their own actions before God, and that a strict moral life had no room for idle pleasure. They greatly disliked theatre and Shakespeare's company of actors would have had many disagreements with the Puritan-influenced government of London.

PUBLIC THEATRES CLOSED

Puritanism was the rising force in English life in the years following Shakespeare's death in 1616. Oliver Cromwell, who ruled the country after the execution of King Charles I in 1649, and his Puritan supporters disapproved of public theatres so much that they closed them down.

There were no public performances in London between 1649 and 1660, when the pleasure-loving King Charles II came to the throne and the theatres opened once more. It is not surprising that *Twelfth Night*, the play about love and 'cakes and ale', in which a kill-joy Puritan was punished, was a popular choice. Samuel Pepys, whose famous diary tells us so much about English life at this time, saw it three times, but hated it:

'... silly ... one of the weakest plays that ever I saw on stage.'

Maybe the actors were playing for easy laughs?

ADAPTING SHAKESPEARE'S ORIGINAL

In 1703 there was an adaptation of the play, called *Love Betrayed*, one of several versions of Shakespeare's plays at that time which simplify the originals, adjusting them for changed tastes. During the eighteenth century there were different attitudes towards Malvolio. In 1741, the Irish actor Charles Macklin drew out the sadness of this lonely figure. On the other hand, a critic writing in 1771 described Malvolio as 'that ridiculous composition of stiff impertinence and uncommon conceit.'

The play was frequently staged in the nineteenth century in the fashionable London theatres. There was even an operatic version which was popular for some years. When a play is well known, actors feel a particular challenge to make their mark – to do something different with a role. In 1865 Kate Terry played both **Viola** and **Sebastian**. Later on her sister, Ellen Terry, gave Viola a wistful and resigned air in a production staged by one of the great actor-managers, Sir Henry Irving.

CRITICISM

Critics writing about eighteenth- and nineteenth-century performances were interested in the leading characters and the actors who played them, but sometimes had problems with the play itself.
Dr Samuel Johnson, writing in the middle of the eighteenth century, praised its 'elegant and easy' style but criticized the play for not being realistic enough. Herbert Beerbohm Tree's production in 1901 aimed for a realistic stage picture – even using real grass!

The set design for Beerbohm Tree's 1901 production at His Majesty's Theatre, London. Real grass was used!

DIRECTING
TWELFTH NIGHT

Henry Irving and Beerbohm Tree were actor-managers. They decided how a play should be staged, and played a leading role in it. From the end of the nineteenth century this changed. Productions began increasingly to be organized by a director who guided the actors' understanding of the characters and made decisions about design, costumes and the use of music. The director asked questions about the meaning and atmosphere of the play. They did not act, but observed and guided the growth of a production.

WILLIAM POEL

At the end of the nineteenth century, William Poel founded the English Stage Society. His aim was to get back to the way the Lord Chamberlain's Men and the King's Men would have performed, although it has to be said his actors were less talented.

Norman Wilkinson's geometric design for a 1912 production at the Savoy Theatre, London, directed by Harley Granville-Barker.

In 1897 they took *Twelfth Night* back to the Middle Temple where John Manningham had seen it in 1602. Men at arms stood around the stage, and even in the corridors leading to the hall. The text was spoken quickly, there was almost no set, and actors wore costumes of Shakespeare's time. But the women's parts were played by actresses, not boys as in the sixteenth century.

HARLEY GRANVILLE-BARKER

Poel's rediscoveries about Shakespeare were taken much further in the next few years by Harley Granville-Barker, who directed *Twelfth Night* in 1912. Rather than historical reproduction, Barker tried to find the essential quality of sixteenth-century style. Gardens and rooms were suggested by formal imitation trees or cut-out archways. Costumes expressed character rather than copying old paintings. Above all, the text sounded loud and clear on an uncluttered stage. Barker's *Twelfth Night* began a tradition of Shakespearean production which has dominated the last eighty years.

FINDING ILLYRIA

For Shakespeare and his audience the name 'Illyria' referred to a real place, what we now know as Croatia. The Elizabethans would have heard stories of pirates, wild rioting and drunkenness there. But Shakespeare applies these travellers' tales of a distant land to his own society. Illyria is a sort of upside-down England. In 1993, Ian Judge, directing the play for the RSC, set it in a quite recognizable Stratford-upon-Avon to make this point even more directly. Where is Illyria? It is where the ordinary is turned upside down and the unexpected breaks through.

In his 1987 production for the RSC, Bill Alexander chose to set the play in a sunny Mediterranean village.

WHICH SEASON OF THE YEAR?

A further question for directors is 'what time of year is it?'. Bill Alexander's 1987 RSC production and Bill Buffery's for Orchard Theatre in Devon in 1988, gave the play a summery Mediterranean setting: hot, sun-drenched, whitewashed buildings under blue skies. In contrast, John Caird's 1983 RSC production had an autumnal feel: the set was dominated by a huge English oak tree shedding its leaves. In his 1979 production at Stratford, Terry Hands opened the play in dark winter which turned to spring as love flourished. Kenneth Branagh's 1988 Renaissance Theatre production was set in winter, emphasizing those characters like **Feste** and **Malvolio** who are left out in the cold at the end.

MUSIC IN *TWELFTH NIGHT*

All of Shakespeare's plays contain songs and other music, but in *Twelfth Night* they play a most important part. They create a world of sadness and loss behind the often delighted confusions of the plot. The subtle use of music was used to create a mood. This was made easier for Shakespeare and his company of actors because they increasingly performed indoors – in court and at royal palaces, on tour in market halls or great houses, and eventually in their own purpose-built threatre, the Blackfriars, in London.

Shakespeare was also no doubt encouraged to make much more use of musical effects by the arrival in the acting company of a brilliant clown, Robert Armin, who had a fine singing voice. Armin would have played Feste in the first performances of *Twelfth Night*.

When William Poel tried to recreate *Twelfth Night* at the end of the nineteenth century, he turned to a musician, Arnold Dolmetsch, who was making a name for himself as an expert on early music. This production used sixteenth- and seventeenth-century instruments, such as the lute and recorders, to accompany the songs.

Directors of more recent versions have explored the music in different ways. In Kenneth Branagh's wintery version for the Renaissance Theatre Company, you could hear snatches of 'The Twelve Days of Christmas'. In John Caird's 1983 production at Stratford, the whole company joined in Feste's final song, 'When that I was and a little tiny boy …' In the 1994 RSC production, director Ian Judge wanted music to run through the whole play, sometimes accompanying the spoken text like film music.

Zoe Wanamaker as Viola and Sarah Berger as Olivia in John Caird's RSC production in 1983.

Director Ian Judge rehearsing with Haydn Gwynne (Olivia), Desmond Barrit (Malvolio) and Tony Britton (Sir Toby Belch) at Stratford, 1994.

THE WORLD OF THE PLAY

As well as making decisions about all aspects of a production, a crucial role of a director is to create the world of the play. *Twelfth Night* is full of interesting characters and lovely songs, asks fascinating questions about love and friendship and raises troubling questions about deception and madness. But above all it is a play about a mood. Everything that happens must bring that into focus.

For most directors since Harley Granville-Barker, the mood has been one of joy and delight constantly undercut by a sense of sadness and loss. The play opens sadly: **Viola** thinks her brother has drowned; **Olivia** is mourning the death of her brother. Into this painful world **Sir Toby Belch** and **Maria** burst, full of jollity.

But even they succumb to the sense of time passing, of nothing lasting for ever. Feste's songs about love and loss express this most clearly. For many directors, in fact, his bitter-sweet mood sums it all up:

'... pleasure must be paid one time or another.'

THE MOOD OF LOVE AND LOSS

Directors search for clear ways of showing this mood of love and loss. They may set the play in autumn or winter, when good times are just a fading memory; they may use music to create a suitable atmosphere; they may encourage costume designers to use muted colours – the reds, golds and browns of autumn, or the blacks, whites and greys of winter. Each of these decisions will help actors and audience alike to enter into and respond to the world of the play.

PLAYING MALVOLIO

Whoever first played **Malvolio** for the Lord Chamberlain's Men must have had a lot of fun. But he was also taking a risk interpreting this biting satire on pompous officials. Someone at court might even have recognized himself! It would have been hard to resist the opportunities for comic effect.

Malvolio is a man who is given a little power and authority which goes to his head. He has to be cut down to size. Modern television situation comedy has lots of fun with very similar characters – those in *Red Dwarf* and *The Brittas Empire*, for example; and Captain Mainwaring, the bank manager turned Home Guard Captain in *Dad's Army*, is in some ways a direct descendant of Malvolio the steward.

SELF-CERTAIN

Malvolio is a wickedly accurate picture of the sort of person who is always right. He is so sure of himself that he has no room for any doubt at all. Of course, he sees that as a great strength. He expects to be obeyed by Olivia's servants. He is rude to all those he thinks are less important than himself – and that means most people! He even begins to imagine he is just the sort of person **Olivia** would want to marry.

He convinces himself that as her husband he would be her master.

But the very self-certainty that makes him shout at **Belch**, **Aguecheek** and **Feste** having a late-night drink, also brings about Malvolio's downfall. Having convinced himself that he is perfect in every way, and that Olivia is attracted to him, he is wide open to the trick **Maria** and the others play on him. Because he cannot doubt himself, and has no sense of humour or imagination, he cannot see the obvious practical joke of the letter left lying in the garden. His pride leads him straight into the trap.

DONALD SINDEN

The most satisfying and interesting performances of Malvolio make him more than simply absurdly proud. There are deeper decisions to be made about his character. How much can Malvolio feel anything for others? How far does he suffer, and so how much should we pity him? Donald Sinden, playing the part in 1969, managed to make him both comic and pitiful in his lonely desire to be loved. There is a tradition that Richard Burbage, the actor in Shakespeare's company who first played Hamlet, Othello and King Lear, was the first Malvolio. If that is true, then maybe Shakespeare intended there to be a serious, even tragic, side to the part.

For Sinden, it was very important that Malvolio had no sense of humour. Because he couldn't laugh at others, he couldn't laugh at himself, and because he couldn't laugh at himself, the trick that is played on him destroys him. He is tormented in prison and at the end he leaves Olivia's house, swearing to be revenged. But for Donald Sinden the threat was an empty one. Malvolio's dignity has been shattered. He has nowhere to go, and nothing else to do. When Donald Sinden's Malvolio left the stage, it was to go and kill himself.

A SOCIAL CLIMBER

Actors want to make the most of the ridiculous aspects they find in the character, especially those surrounding Malvolio's social pretensions.

He is a social climber who fantasizes about marrying Olivia because she would be his passport to high status and a life of privilege, which he is sure he deserves.

Laurence Olivier chose to bring out this aspect of Malvolio by giving him a 'posh' accent. In fact decisions about how Malvolio should speak are very important as a way of communicating his social position. Desmond Barritt played him in 1993 using his own accent – Welsh. This made Malvolio an outsider: he would always be isolated because he would always sound different from everyone else. Barritt's performance was richly comic: this Malvolio was a vain man standing on the shifting sands of his own dignity.

Desmond Barritt's
Malvolio, RSC, 1994.

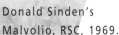

Donald Sinden's
Malvolio, RSC, 1969.

PLAYING THE LORDS
(AND LADY) OF MISRULE

In Shakespeare's time, celebrations at Christmas were often led by a Lord of Misrule, whose job was to make sure that the festivities were full of fun and mischief. In *Twelfth Night* this role is taken by **Sir Toby Belch**, **Sir Andrew Aguecheek** and **Maria**. In Ian Judge's 1993 RSC production, Bille Brown played Sir Andrew as a simple clown, entirely innocent and naïve. Brown has played Falstaff and **Malvolio** and believes that 'the magical humour of Shakespeare's comedy is always underscored by bitterness and pain …' His Aguecheek was both funny and vulnerable, fluttering around Sir Toby one moment, going weak-kneed at the thought of a duel with **Cesario** the next.

Sir Toby Belch (John Thaw),
Sir Andrew Aguecheek (Daniel Massey)
and Feste (Richard O'Callaghan) in
John Caird's 1983 production.

He sums up his experience of the play:

'… the romantic characters become funnier and happier as the play goes on. But those characters who start as comic become exhausted objects of pity. It's as though there are two forces moving in opposite directions in the play'.

INNOCENCE AND EXPERIENCE

Twelfth Night is a play of youth and age, innocence and experience. The comedy comes from the oldest characters of all, the Lords and Lady of Misrule, and their victim, Malvolio. They all have some connection with **Olivia**: Sir Toby is her uncle, Maria her personal servant, and Sir Andrew thinks he's in love with her. They are all energetic singers, dancers and tricksters, even if Sir Andrew is often a step behind and the object of Maria's and Sir Toby's jokes as well.

But they all go too far and the humour first turns nasty and then simply runs out. Maria is perhaps angry and resentful at Malvolio's attempts to dominate the household and take away her own special relationship with Olivia.

As the steward of Olivia's household, Malvolio is powerful and responsible but definitely a servant. The issue of social position fuels the dislike between him and Sir Toby: 'Art [are you] any more than a steward?' Bill Wallis played Sir Toby in an RSC production in 1991 and brought out some of his less attractive characteristics. This was an ageing, tired, cynical man shamelessly milking Sir Andrew for all the money he could get. Sir Andrew was played by Tim McInnerney as young and painfully gullible.

A Happy Ending?

Twelfth Night is the last day of Christmas, a time when the decorations are finally taken down and life begins to return to normal after the festivities. In *Twelfth Night*, Shakespeare's last real comedy, the mood is always one of time running out and boisterous mischief having to be put away so that real life can take over again. The audience is told that Sir Toby and Maria have been married, though it is hard to believe that their marriage will be as loving or happy as those of Olivia and **Sebastian**, **Viola** and **Orsino**. Sir Andrew, too, goes home a poorer, but probably not much wiser man. Bille Brown is right when he says that the comic characters become 'exhausted objects of pity'.

Abigail McKern (Maria), Richard Briers (Malvolio), Caroline Langrishe (Olivia) and Frances Barber (Viola), in the 1988 Renaissance Theatre production.

PLAYING
VIOLA AND FESTE

Viola is one of several Shakespearean heroines who sets off on an adventure disguised as a boy. The complications of this were far greater for actors and audiences in Shakespeare's time than they are today. Then, there were no professional women actors and all female parts were played by boys. For the boy actor who played Viola, the experience must have been complex. A boy playing a girl playing a boy! It is rather like those sets of Chinese boxes in which opening one reveals another, and so on. What is more, the **Cesario** 'box' attracts the love of another woman, whilst the Viola 'box' is in love with **Orsino**. An actor needs great flexibility and quick-wittedness to be in the right box at the right time!

This challenge has attracted all the greatest actresses. Many accounts of earlier twentieth-century Violas show a search for a thoughtful, even subdued mood. This seems to have been true of Ellen Terry at the turn of the century and of Vivien Leigh in the 1930s. Peggy Ashcroft played Viola twice, in 1938 and 1950. She was praised for her charm and wit on the first occasion, but some felt she lacked sadness on the second. Judi Dench played Viola with great success in 1969.

The interplay of liveliness and sadness in her performance was one of its most remarkable, and satisfying, features.

A performance by Dorothy Tutin at Stratford in 1958 captured the many moods of the character very well. Critics praised her as,

'the absolute Viola, all gentleness, courage, steadfastness and fear.'

Viola/Cesario (Dorothy Tutin) reunited with her twin brother Sebastian (Ian Holm) in Peter Hall's production in 1958.

PLAYING FESTE

Robert Armin, the first actor to play **Feste**, was a singer and musician and a witty performer of comic roles. He was also the first Fool in *King Lear* a few years later. Like Feste, that Fool is an 'allowed fool' too: a court jester; a funny man with a licence to tell the truth, however painful; a man who keeps his wits when everyone around him is losing theirs. This is Feste's job, and it makes many demands on any actor who plays the role.

The importance of casting the right actor for the part is crucial. He must be able to sing and to act across a wide range of moods. Max Adrian played a worldly-wise, rather bitter Feste in Peter Hall's production in 1958. He delivered his songs sarcastically. By contrast in 1993 at Stratford, Derek Griffiths, with his fine singing voice, began from Feste's musical skill. Part of this Feste's isolation was the fact that he was an artist, only really able to express himself through music.

Anton Lesser played Feste in the Renaissance Theatre production in 1988, and fortunately his performance was recorded on video-tape. He was a man clinging on to sanity; only being a fool seemed to stop him from going mad in this topsy-turvy world (just like Lear's Fool). He arrived at **Olivia's** house in a snowstorm carrying a suitcase. The audience was left in no doubt that this Feste loved Olivia, one of the loves in the play which is never returned. At the end he left Illyria once more. He sang his song, picked up his suitcase and left the stage in the snow, closing the gate of Olivia's garden behind him. The winter revels were over and new starts had to be made. The happiness of the loving couples at the end of this production was cut across by the sadness of those who remained alone, still searching for the 'other half' to make them whole.

Anton Lesser was a sad and lonely Feste in the wintery Renaissance Theatre production in 1988.

Index

CONTENTS

INTRODUCTION

By 1596 or 1597, when *The Merchant of Venice* was probably written and first performed, William Shakespeare was an experienced man of the theatre and a famous and skilful writer. He had already written *Romeo and Juliet*, *A Midsummer Night's Dream* and *Richard III*, for example, and had published the long poems *Venus and Adonis* and *The Rape of Lucrece*, which brought him to the attention of possible wealthy patrons. On 22 July 1598 'a book of *The Merchant of Venice* or otherwise called *The Jew of Venice*' was entered in the Stationer's Register (an official list of all printed books), probably in an attempt by Shakespeare's acting company, The Lord Chamberlain's Men, to stop it from being printed by anyone else.

SOURCES

Just as with so many of his plays, Shakespeare took ideas from a lot of different places to make a new and fascinating story. There is a tale in a book called *Il Pecorone* by the Italian writer Ser Giovanni, which gave Shakespeare some basic ideas for his play.

Il Pecorone – which means 'the big sheep' or 'the fool' – was published in 1558. As it wasn't translated into English, Shakespeare quite possibly read it in Italian. But the idea of the three caskets, which Portia's suitors must choose between, doesn't come from this story. It appears in a lot of tales, and Shakespeare probably found it in Italian or English collections of stories such as Boccaccio's *Decameron* or John Gower's *Confessio Amantis*.

In writing a play about a Jew, Shakespeare was following a trend.

William Shakespeare, an oil painting, probably by John Taylor and dated 1610. It hangs in the National Portrait Gallery.

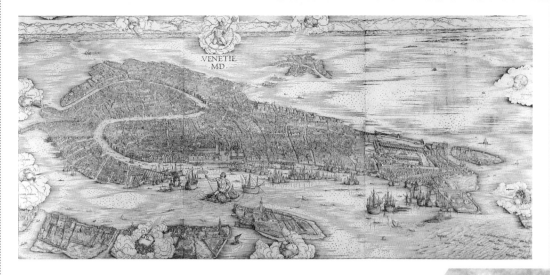

Part of a woodcut said to be by
Jacopo de' Barbari, 1500, showing
a bird's-eye view of Venice.

Christopher Marlowe had had a great success in 1589 with *The Jew of Malta*, and Shakespeare may well have got the idea of a Jewish girl marrying a Christian (as **Jessica** marries **Lorenzo**) from that play. There were other plays about Jews at this time too.

PREJUDICE

Most Londoners would never have seen a Jew. People in the once thriving Jewish community had been expelled as long ago as 1290, after many years of being forced to wear a yellow badge to mark them out. Prejudice grew out of ignorance. Although a few had returned, including a pocket of Portuguese Jews, on the whole they were seen as strange and different, and hated as the people held responsible for the death of Jesus.

Shakespeare's **Shylock** is a much more complex character than Marlowe's Jew, Barabas.

But some people believe the play is deeply anti-Semitic. They feel it is a play which should no longer be performed because it repeats and reinforces prejudices about Jews. Others see Shylock as a tragic figure, trapped by prejudice and driven to revenge by the treatment he gets.

The Merchant of Venice is one of Shakespeare's most disturbing creations. The playwright's insight into human nature never fails to surprise and puzzle his audience. The play is full of joy and energy but it is never far away from darkness and pain. It deals with serious matters, and yet can be wonderfully funny. Above all it asks questions about trust and tolerance which remain as fresh and as challenging now as when it was written.

THE CHARACTERS

Antonio is a merchant of Venice, who borrows money from Shylock to lend to his friend Bassanio.

Bassanio is Antonio's friend. He is courting Portia.

Leonardo is Bassanio's servant.

Lorenzo is a friend of Antonio and Bassanio. He elopes with Shylock's daughter, Jessica.

Graziano is also a friend of Antonio and Bassanio. He will marry Nerissa, Portia's maid.

Salerio and **Solanio** are friends of Antonio and Bassanio.

Shylock is a Jew of Venice, who lends money to Antonio.

Jessica is Shylock's daughter. She runs away to become a Christian and marry Lorenzo, taking Shylock's money and jewels with her.

Tubal is another Jew of Venice.

Launcelot Gobbo with his old father in a 1981 Royal Shakespeare Company (RSC) production at Stratford.

Shylock (Anthony Sher), Antonio
(John Carlisle) and Bassanio
(Nicholas Farrell) in Bill Alexander's
production at Stratford, 1987.

Launcelot Gobbo is Shylock's servant. He later leaves Shylock and becomes Bassanio's servant.

Old Gobbo is Launcelot's father.

Portia is an heiress who lives at Belmont near Venice. Before he died, her father insisted she must only marry the man who chose of three caskets (one of gold, one of silver, one of lead) the one with her portrait in.

Nerissa is Portia's maid, who will marry Graziano.

Balthasar and **Stefano** are Portia's servants.

The Prince of Aragon and **The Prince of Morocco** come to Belmont wishing to marry Portia and try to solve the riddle of the caskets.

The Duke of Venice presides at the trial of Antonio.

There are also a **jailer**, **attendants**, **servants** and **magnificoes** (lords) **of Venice**.

WHAT HAPPENS
IN THE PLAY

Antonio, a merchant of Venice, is telling **Salerio** and **Solanio** that he is sad. They ask if he is anxious about the safety of his ships, due in to Venice at any time, but he denies it. They then ask if he's in love but Antonio dismisses the idea. **Bassanio**, **Lorenzo** and **Graziano** arrive and after Salerio and Solanio have gone, Graziano does his best to cheer up Antonio, but without success. Soon he and Lorenzo leave, arranging to meet them all again that evening.

Bassanio tells Antonio that he is in love with **Portia**, whose father has recently died. He is in despair as he hasn't the money to compete with the rich men who want to marry her. He asks Antonio for a loan – although he has borrowed a good deal from him already. Bassanio promises that if he marries Portia, Antonio will get back everything he has ever borrowed. But Antonio says that until his ships arrive safely he has no money to lend to Bassanio.

In Belmont, Portia and **Nerissa** are discussing the men who are coming to ask for Portia's hand in marriage. Portia only likes Bassanio. News comes that the **Princes of Morocco** and **Aragon** have arrived.

A MERRY BOND

Meanwhile, back in Venice, Bassanio has approached **Shylock** for a loan. Shylock agrees, but only if someone will repay the loan, with interest, if Bassanio cannot. Bassanio asks Antonio to meet Shylock and a deal is struck: if Bassanio is unable to repay, then Shylock will cut off a pound of Antonio's flesh. Shylock doesn't seem to be serious, calling it 'a merry bond', and in any case Antonio is full of confidence:

'In this there can be no dismay.
My ships come home a month
before the day.'

The Prince of Morocco arrives to woo Portia. She tells him the bargain: he must choose of three caskets (gold, silver and lead) the one which contains her portrait.

'Who chooseth me shall get as much as he deserves.' The Prince of Aragon decides on the silver casket in the RSC's 1984 production, directed by John Caird.

If he chooses the right one, he can marry her and share her wealth; if he makes the wrong choice, he must agree never to marry anyone. He accepts the deal.

Meanwhile in Venice, Shylock's servant **Launcelot Gobbo** is trying to decide whether to stay with the Jew or run away. He battles with his conscience and decides to leave. His old, blind father arrives. Launcelot asks for an introduction to Bassanio, whom he wants to serve instead of Shylock. Bassanio now joins them and agrees that Launcelot should become his servant. After the Gobbos have gone, Graziano appears and begs to be allowed to go with Bassanio to Belmont.

JESSICA RUNS AWAY

Launcelot Gobbo says farewell to Shylock's daughter, **Jessica**, who gives him a letter for Lorenzo. She is planning to run away, marry him and become a Christian. Lorenzo gets the letter and with his friends plans to take Jessica away that very night while Shylock is away from home.

That evening Shylock goes out, trusting Jessica to look after the house. Soon after, Lorenzo and his friends arrive, wearing masks as if for a party. Jessica goes with them, taking Shylock's money and jewels.

Once more the scene changes to Belmont where the Prince of Morocco has to make his choice between the caskets of gold, silver and lead. He chooses the gold casket – he's wrong, and a message inside reminds him:

'All that glisters is not gold.'

Later that night in Venice Shylock discovers his betrayal by Jessica, to the pleasure of Antonio's friends, while in Belmont another suitor arrives – the Prince of Aragon. He too makes his choice – silver – but he, too, is wrong. The Prince leaves, and a message comes for Portia that Bassanio has arrived.

DISASTER FOR ANTONIO

News arrives in Venice that one of Antonio's ships has been wrecked. His friends, Salerio and Solanio, are at the Rialto (where merchants met to make deals and obtain information about trade) when Shylock arrives. Hearing that Antonio has lost his fortune and will not be able to repay Bassanio's loan, Shylock decides to hold Antonio to his word, saying:

'Let him look to his bond.'

Salerio tries to laugh off the taking of a pound of flesh; but Shylock is out for revenge. He feels he has been insulted by Antonio, as by all the Christian merchants of Venice. To make things worse, they have taken Jessica away from him. He will have the flesh: 'If it will feed nothing else, it will feed my revenge.' All the pent-up sense of the wrong done to his people overflows:

'I am a Jew ... If you prick us do we not bleed? If you tickle us do we not laugh? If you poison us do we not die? And if you wrong us shall we not revenge?'

As Antonio's friends leave, another Jew, **Tubal**, arrives with the news that more of Antonio's ships have been sunk: he is ruined.

'What, what, what? ill luck, ill luck?' Shylock, played by Ian MacDiarmid, hears the news of the loss of Antonio's ships from Tubal.

BASSANIO'S CHOICE

Meanwhile in Belmont Bassanio is preparing to choose a casket. Although Portia is sure she loves him, she has sworn not to give away the secret. He must choose without any help from her. With much care he rejects the beautiful gold and silver caskets and picks the simple lead one. He is right. The portrait is inside with a message telling him to

'Turn you where your lady is, And claim her with a loving kiss.'

Antonio's friends arrive with Jessica and give the bad news about the merchant's losses. Portia tells Bassanio that he should go back to Venice. She will give him the money he needs to help Antonio.

In Venice Antonio is in prison. The merchant tries to renegotiate but Shylock refuses:

'I'll have no speaking. I will have my bond.'

Back in Belmont Portia has decided to help Bassanio: she will disguise herself as a lawyer and use her skill and knowledge to defend Antonio in court.

JUSTICE?

The day of the court hearing has arrived. The **Duke of Venice** tries to comfort Antonio, who is resigned to his fate. Shylock now comes into the court. The Duke invites him to work out a compromise, to show mercy:

'We all expect a gentle answer, Jew.'

Shylock, however, is firm. He argues that he must take his stand on the law. He repeats that a man's word is his bond. It is the duty of government and law to ensure that he pays what he owes. Bassanio offers to pay the money, and more. Shylock has lent three thousand ducats; he can have six thousand. But Shylock rejects it: not even for six times six thousand ducats will he compromise.

Portia arrives, dressed as Balthasar, a lawyer from Rome. She brings Shylock and Antonio forward. She accepts that Antonio has failed to meet the agreed terms.

She asks Shylock to show mercy. He refuses. He refuses to accept the money from Bassanio. Portia/Balthasar now seems to be on Shylock's side. To the fury of the court and Shylock's satisfaction, she gives him the right to the pound of flesh. Just as he has taken a knife to cut it off, she stops him. She points out that the bond speaks of flesh, but not blood. The law protects citizens of Venice from plots against their life. So Shylock cannot shed a drop of Antonio's blood – simply to consider doing so is punishable.

Shylock recognizes he is defeated by the very terms of strict justice on which, in his own anger, he had taken a stand. He tries to bargain, but all his offers are rejected. He leaves the court a beaten man: forced to agree that all his possessions will go to Jessica and Lorenzo, but worst of all, forced to become a Christian.

The trial of Antonio. Shylock (David Suchet) confronts Portia/Balthasar (Sinead Cusack) in the RSC production in 1981.

THE RING

After Shylock has gone, Bassanio thanks Portia/Balthasar and offers to give her a token of their gratitude. The lawyer asks Bassanio for a ring that Portia has given him. Reluctantly he hands it over. The lawyer takes the ring and leaves.

BELMONT

In Belmont, Jessica and Lorenzo are in the garden. It is night and they are enjoying its romantic beauty. They are disturbed, first by **Stefano**, Portia's servant, telling them his mistress will be back before dawn, and then by Launcelot Gobbo, who says that Bassanio, his master, will be coming in the morning.

When they are alone again, Lorenzo calls for music:

> *'With sweetest touches pierce your mistress' ear*
> *And draw her home with music.'*

Jessica and Lorenzo lie together, listening, bewitched by its sweetness and the starry night.

Portia and Nerissa arrive, quickly followed by Bassanio, Antonio and their friends. Graziano has fallen in love with Nerissa and has come to woo her.

The men, of course, have not guessed that Balthasar the lawyer was really Portia, and when she asks Bassanio about the ring, he lies, saying he has lost it. But Portia shows it to him, saying the lawyer gave it to her. And Nerissa says that she has been with the lawyer's clerk. Both Graziano and Bassanio are shocked: have the women been unfaithful?

TYING UP LOOSE ENDS

Portia now ties up all the loose ends. She admits that she and Nerissa were in Venice in disguise. She also tells Antonio that his ships have indeed arrived safely and he is still a rich man. Nerissa shows Shylock's agreement to Lorenzo and Jesssica – they will have his wealth.

All seems to end well enough, though the audience can hardly forget Shylock's pain and the shocks and surprises so many of the men have had. Antonio's light-heartedness about the deal with Shylock has brought him near to death. Bassanio's selfishness in wanting money has put his friend Antonio in danger, and Portia has shown how mean he can be, giving away the ring she has given him to keep.

'How sweet the moonlight sleeps upon this bank ...'
Lorenzo (Mark Lewis Jones) and Jessica (Kate Duchêne) enjoy the beauty of the night in the garden at Belmont, RSC, 1993

MERCHANTS
AND MONEYLENDERS

I n 1598 the play was described as '… *The Merchant of Venice* or otherwise called *The Jew of Venice*'. It was printed in 1600 as *The Comical History of the Merchant of Venice*. The various titles give an indication of the range of ideas in the play. Is the central character **Antonio**, the merchant, or **Shylock**, the Jew, who is a moneylender? Is it right to call the play a comedy? While some characters find love and happiness, others go off to loneliness and despair. Even those who do live 'happily ever after' have had painful experiences which make them sadder and wiser. Above all the play is about trade, making deals and taking chances, honesty and trust, and justice and mercy.

THE MERCHANTS AND THE JEWS OF VENICE

For hundreds of years the harbours of Venice on the east coast of Italy had been at the centre of trade between Europe and the Orient. Venetian merchants bought silks and spices (especially pepper), jewellery, fine pottery, silver, dyes and medicines from Turkey, the Middle East, and even China. They sold them at a great profit to the countries of northern Europe. Christian merchants like Antonio needed to borrow money to set up the trading expeditions that would make them rich.

Although the Jews of Europe were barred from many ways of earning a living, they were allowed to lend money for profit (called usury), and merchants turned to Jews when they needed loans. The moneylenders charged interest on the loan so merchants had to pay back more than they originally borrowed, but this would easily have been covered by the profits they made from their trade.

An illustration of a Venetian nobleman promising to keep the laws of Venice, from a book called *Giuramento of the Procurator Girolomo Zane*. The artist is unknown, but the picture is dated about 1570. It is illuminated on vellum.

Christians relied on Jews for a supply of money, but could Jews rely on Christians? Jews were tolerated as moneylenders but they were quickly blamed when things went wrong. They had little protection in law, and public opinion was against them. Does Shylock feel he must drive a hard bargain because he can't trust the merchant to keep the deal? And why does Antonio accept 'a pound of flesh' as the terms of the loan? Perhaps he so much wants to help **Bassanio**, is so sure of the return of his fleet of ships, and is so scornful of Shylock, that he doesn't take it seriously.

The play is about a Christian and a Jew, a merchant and a moneylender. Shakespeare shows us two men each of whom has something the other wants. Shylock has the money Antonio needs; Antonio has the respect and social standing that Shylock, as a Jew, cannot have.

THE MERCHANT OF STRATFORD

William Shakespeare's father, John, was a merchant in Stratford. Not only did he make high quality white leather goods, he also traded in other things – buying cheaply and selling at a profit. John Shakespeare was a moneylender as well, at a time when usury was still illegal, although essential for trading. In the early 1590s, John's fortunes declined and he was afraid of being arrested for debt. When Shakespeare wrote about trade and moneylending in *The Merchant of Venice,* he was exploring a world he knew from the inside, and was aware of its risks as well as its glamour.

Portia (Penny Downie) and Bassanio (Owen Teale) in David Thacker's production for the RSC, 1993.

'THEN MUST THE JEW BE MERCIFUL?'

When Antonio is unable to repay the money he has borrowed, Shylock takes him into a court of law for justice. The battle between Shylock and Balthasar (**Portia** in disguise) is often seen as a struggle between the Jewish concern for 'the letter of the law' and the Christian willingness to show mercy. This is too simple. When Shylock insists on justice and rejects any suggestion of compromise, he is taking his stand on a particular interpretation of the law – he had a deal with Antonio; Antonio has defaulted; the bond must be repaid. Shylock even tells the **Duke** that any compromise would ruin the reputation of Venice as a place in which to do business.

On a strict reading of the law, Shylock has a case, but Portia/Balthasar argues that if the law is seen only as a way of settling disputes between two individuals, then the strongest will win. Mercy is about compassion and compromise, but above all it is the right of a court to mitigate: that is, a court cannot overturn the law, but it can try to lessen its extreme effects. Mercy is as much a part of honest dealing as is the demand for the pound of flesh.

Shylock (played by Antony Sher) is cruelly baited by the Christians of Venice in Bill Alexander's 1987 RSC production.

SHYLOCK'S BETRAYAL

Why does Shylock insist on justice according to the letter of the law? Some productions of the play have insisted on the anti-Semitic interpretation that all Jews are wicked, and therefore Shylock is too. Others, accepting that this sort of generalization is wrong, and based on unthinking prejudice, have seen Shylock as a wicked man, who happens to be a Jew.

But some have looked more deeply. Shylock, as a Jew in a Christian city, has had to fight for survival. His experience has told him not to trust anyone. He says that Christian merchants insulted him even when they wanted to borrow money from him. And then his daughter **Jessica** betrays him, eloping with **Lorenzo**, a Christian. Maybe Shylock, hurt and angry at the loss of his daughter and the jewels she took with her, wants to get his own back.

VENICE AND BELMONT

Although much of the play is set in the bustling public world of Venice, it is contrasted with Belmont, Portia's home outside the city. This is a private, intimate place of love, joy and music. Lovers or would-be lovers come to Belmont; it could hardly be more different from Venice. And yet, Shakespeare overturns our certainties. Portia is beautiful, intelligent and witty.

By the terms of her late father's will, though, she must marry the man who makes the right choice in a test. She is like a piece of merchandise herself, waiting to be claimed.

Portia's suitors in Belmont, the **Princes of Morocco** and **Aragon**, have to take the sort of risk any merchant must, making unseen bids for goods, as they guess in which of the caskets Portia's portrait is to be found. Like inexperienced traders, they are conned by outside appearances, choosing the gold and silver boxes, learning to their cost that 'all that glisters is not gold …'

Bassanio chooses the lead casket because, like a clever merchant, he is prepared to take a calculated risk. Bassanio is successful and Portia gets the man she wants, but Shakespeare doesn't let the audience forget that in his time women were the property of their husbands, no matter how clever or rich they were.

And Portia is certainly clever. She can outsmart the Venetians in the law courts. She cynically traps Bassanio by getting him to give her the ring, showing how far he has still to go before he can be trusted. Only Shylock is a real match for her, but she backs him into a position where he must either die or lose everything. In the law court and in Belmont, too, Portia shows up the men as often selfish, arrogant and foolish.

THE MERCHANT OF VENICE
ON STAGE

We do not know exactly when or where *The Merchant of Venice* was first performed. It is mentioned by a law student called Francis Meres in his book *Palladis Tamia* in 1598. The printed version of 1600 says that it has been 'divers times [often] acted by the Lord Chamberlain's Servants'. The first recorded performance was on Sunday 10 February 1605 when King James I saw it performed. The King must have liked what he saw because he asked for another performance two days later.

It is likely that *The Merchant of Venice* was still performed after Shakespeare's death in 1616 but the next certain date is 1701, when a much rewritten version, called *The Jew of Venice*, was played at Drury Lane in London. **Shylock** was a figure of fun, played by the comic actor Thomas Doggett, and **Bassanio** became the central character. Much of Shakespeare's text was cut out or greatly changed.

CHARLES MACKLIN

The Jew of Venice was performed for forty years, until 14 February 1741.

On that day, the Irish actor Charles Macklin strode on to the stage at Drury Lane in a restored version of Shakespeare's play, 136 years almost to the day since its last known full performance. Macklin wiped away the memory of Shylock as a comic character. His performance so disturbed King George II that he suggested the whole House of Commons should be sent to see it to give them a fright.

Macklin's Shylock was a vicious villain out for revenge, growling out his lines, glaring at his enemies with eyes that were 'like a tiger peeping out of the bush', according to a fellow actor. He played Shylock for nearly fifty years until, just before his ninetieth birthday, his memory failed him during a performance, and he retired from the stage.

Edmund Kean as Shylock, a man of dignity even in defeat.

EDMUND KEAN

On 26 January 1814 a little known actor stood in the wings at Drury Lane waiting to go on stage as Shylock. Other actors shook their heads doubtfully. He wasn't wearing a dirty gown and a red wig – didn't he know this was how Shylock was supposed to appear? But Edmund Kean, making his first London appearance, had other ideas. If his Shylock was a villain, he would have humanity too, a man of dignity even in defeat. Playgoers were struck by the glare of contempt with which he fixed **Graziano** as he left the stage for the last time after the trial.

Kean's Shylock was proud to be a Jew. Maybe as a man who felt persecuted and misunderstood himself, Kean recognized Shylock's own struggle for survival among those who hated him.

HENRY IRVING

If Macklin rescued Shakespeare's revenging villain, and Kean rediscovered the human face of Shylock, Henry Irving, one of the greatest actors of the nineteenth century, presented a Jew in almost complete command of himself and his feelings. Although his control broke down when **Jessica** ran away, by the trial scene it was completely regained as he pursued his plan for revenge with ice-cold restraint.

One critic gives a picture of Irving's Shylock at the trial, listening 'with the horrible stillness and fascination of the rattlesnake'. Throughout, Irving wanted to show how Shylock was driven to revenge by the prejudice and hatred of those around him. This Jew was bearing the weight of the sorrows of all his people – the victim, exhausted by suffering.

Henry Irving as Shylock at the Lyceum Theatre, London, 1879.

DIRECTING
THE MERCHANT OF VENICE

Ever since Charles Macklin brought Shakespeare's text back on to the stage in 1741, *The Merchant of Venice* has remained a favourite with audiences. They have wanted to see great actors and actresses as **Shylock** and **Portia**, and the actors and actresses have wanted to show their skills in these demanding parts. In the eighteenth and nineteenth centuries the leading actor would make decisions about scenery, costumes and even the exits and entrances of other actors. In the twentieth century this job has increasingly been taken by the director, who guides the work of everyone else, bringing a sense of unity and meaning to a production.

Bassanio played by Owen Teale in the steel-framed set designed by Shelagh Keegan at the RSC, 1993.

TRAGEDY OR COMEDY?

As they work on a play, directors and actors have to ask questions about it, and the decisions they reach can make an enormous difference to what an audience will see and hear. One of the first things that has to be decided is whether it is a comedy or a tragedy. Shakespeare's own actors called it a comedy, but we don't know what their production looked like or how it came across to an audience. Many people think that the part of Shylock in Shakespeare's company was played by the great tragic actor Richard Burbage (who also played Hamlet, Othello and Macbeth), but some scholars have suggested it was in fact played by the comedian Will Kemp (who probably played Bottom in *A Midsummer Night's Dream*). What the Chamberlain's Men decided about casting (which actor played what part) would have made a real difference to the play.

In 1709 Nicholas Rowe prepared
an edition of Shakespeare's plays.
Writing about *The Merchant of
Venice*, he said:

*'... we have seen ... the part of
the Jew performed by an
excellent comedian yet I ... think
it was designed tragically by the
author. There appears in it such a
deadly spirit of revenge, such a savage
fierceness ... and such ... cruelty and
mischief, as cannot agree either with
the style or characters of comedy.'*

Most actors and directors now agree.

DESIGNING THE PLAY

Directors and designers need to
agree about the ideas in the play and
how these can best be expressed
visually. In the nineteenth century no
expense would have been spared in
creating scenery that showed Venice
with its canals and bridges, and
Belmont set in a beautiful garden.
Gradually tastes have changed and
designers increasingly began to
'suggest' Venice or Belmont – a
bridge perhaps, or the three caskets
of gold, silver and lead.

Some directors and designers have
looked for modern parallels. These
have sometimes been vicious: in
1943 the Burgtheater in Vienna
performed the play as a way of
celebrating the destruction of the
Jews by the Nazis. The Shylock of
Werner Krauss was a brutal caricature
played for the nastiest of laughs.

When David Thacker directed the
play for the RSC in Stratford in 1993,
he drew out the similarities between
the commercial world of sixteenth-
century Venice and the financial
institutions of modern London.
David Thacker and his designer
Shelagh Keegan created a set of
chrome and steel scaffolding.
Characters wore designer suits and
carried lap-tops. Everything was
calculated to bring into focus the
idea that money can drive people to
do terrible things to one another.

THE TEXT OF THE PLAY

Directors and actors also have to make choices about the words they will speak. This might seem strange. Surely we all know what Shakespeare wrote? But nearly all the plays were printed in two early versions: Quartos, which appeared in Shakespeare's lifetime and the Folio, published in 1623, seven years after his death.

While the Folio texts were probably the versions that were regularly performed, the Quartos came from a range of sources. Some – the Quarto of *Hamlet* for instance – were probably based on actors' memories. Others, including the Quarto of *The Merchant of Venice* which was printed in 1600, were taken from working scripts, maybe even Shakespeare's own. There are many detailed differences between the texts in the Folio and the Quarto, and decisions have to be made about which to use.

Other choices about the text can be more controversial. When David Thacker was preparing the script for the 1993 production at Stratford, he decided to cut some lines to help the characters develop their roles more sympathetically. Shylock's line 'I hate him for he is a Christian' was taken out, as were Portia's lines about the **Prince of Morocco**, which seem racist today.

On the other hand, when Bill Alexander directed the play at Stratford in 1987 with Antony Sher as Shylock, they wanted to drive home the anti-Semitic and racist attitudes of all the Christians, including Portia. So they left in her comments about the black Prince of Morocco which, as they were delivered to **Nerissa** who was played on this occasion by a black actress, were shocking in their unthinking racism.

Bill Alexander's production was remarkable for the viciousness of its Venetians. The upper-class yobs like **Solanio** and **Graziano** could accept Nerissa as honorary white and **Jessica** as honorary Christian, while laughing at Morocco and constantly spitting at Shylock.

The title page from the first Quarto of *The Merchant of Venice*, 1600.

MUSIC AND *THE MERCHANT*

Music plays a key role in many of Shakespeare's plays and is particularly important in *The Merchant of Venice*. In Shakespeare's day music was seen as an expression of harmony, of things fitting together. Elizabethans believed that the planets themselves moved in harmony; music copied and expressed this cosmic good order. Music in a Shakespeare play is not there to fill in the gaps between scenes – beautiful music indicates peace and love.

Belmont is a place of music. When **Lorenzo** and Jessica are waiting for Portia to return from Venice, they call for music. As it is played, Lorenzo speaks of the night and the stars, and the heavenly music only angels hear:

> **'There's not the smallest orb which thou behold'st But in his motion like an angel sings ...'**

Within the play as a whole it is a moment of rest and calm after the trial, before Portia and the others come back to Belmont.

Directors need to be alert to the many musical clues. For example, in the same speech Lorenzo concludes that 'the man that hath no music in himself' cannot be trusted. Is he referring to Shylock? This idea was developed when David Calder played Shylock in the 1993 production at Stratford – we saw him at home listening to classical music on a hi-fi. The assumptions were overturned: this Jew could appreciate beauty.

Shylock (David Calder) at home with Jessica (Kate Duchêne), Stratford, 1993.

PLAYING SHYLOCK

For more than 250 years, **Shylock** has been a role against which many great actors have tested themselves. Some have shown him as an out-and-out villain; others, especially since Edmund Kean and Henry Irving took the role in the nineteenth century, have found in the Jew of Venice a complex figure, driven to revenge by insults and the loss of his daughter.

Directors, critics, actors and their audiences are constantly asking: what did Shakespeare intend? Did he think Shylock was a villain or a hero? Should he be played for laughs? What should we be most aware of – his difference from the other characters, his Jewishness perhaps; or his similarity to them, the feelings he shares, the world of trade of which they are all a part?

ANTONY SHER

One of the most villainous of recent Shylocks was that of Antony Sher in Bill Alexander's 1987 production for the RSC. At one level he seemed a caricature Jew, a man proclaiming his difference by what he wore and how he spoke. But Sher wanted the play to be 'a comment on second-class citizens everywhere', and if his Shylock behaved badly in his lust for revenge it was because he was driven to it by the much worse behaviour of his opponents. It was as if an outsider is forced to be different in order to survive.

Laurence Olivier playing Shylock in Jonathan Miller's production at the National Theatre in 1970.

Antony Sher as a flamboyant Shylock at Stratford in 1987.

LAURENCE OLIVIER

How to move from being an accepted part of the Venetian economy to being an outcast is always a crucial matter for an actor playing Shylock. Some, like Laurence Olivier in Jonathan Miller's 1970 production at the National Theatre, see Shylock as an outsider trying to get in. Olivier showed a man imitating, often with comic results, upper-class Christian behaviour but in the end discovering that they were bigots and frauds. This Shylock wanted desperately to be accepted and only turned on the Christians when he discovered how completely they rejected him.

PATRICK STEWART

When Patrick Stewart played Shylock in John Barton's 1978 RSC production, the actor and director came to the conclusion that Shylock is 'an outsider who happens to be a Jew'. They concentrated on his universality – the characteristics he might share with others. So this Shylock was an unlikeable man: he treated **Jessica** badly; he could be arrogant and unforgiving when he thought he was winning, but when losing would do anything to survive – even laughing along with **Graziano**'s jokes in the trial! Patrick Stewart's Shylock was a tragic figure, brought down by his own failings, who just happened to be a Jew.

DAVID SUCHET

John Barton directed the play again in 1980, at Stratford, and this time David Suchet, playing Shylock, explored what it meant to be an outsider *because* he is a Jew. For Suchet, the Jewish element was 'unavoidable and very important'. He also recognized that Shylock presents another challenge to an actor: he is on stage for only seven scenes and behaves very differently in each one. Many actors try to iron out these differences to get a consistent character, but David Suchet believed that it was important to be inconsistent – 'to play each scene for what it was'. This way you built up a much more complex picture of the character as each new piece of the jigsaw slotted into place.

DAVID CALDER

For David Calder as Shylock in David Thacker's 1993 production for the RSC, the play draws a picture of an intolerant society which the Jew challenges. Shylock knows that **Antonio** hates him but says, in effect, 'We can work together, do business together, and perhaps a friendship could grow.' Shylock puts himself on the line in the name of racial and cultural tolerance. It is only after Jessica leaves him that he comes to believe this is impossible. The tragedy is of a man whose attempts to build bridges are rejected by the society in which he lives until all he has left is revenge.

PLAYING PORTIA

There are three great challenges for any actress playing **Portia**. First of all, she has to live in two different worlds: beautiful Belmont and money-making Venice. Second, for much of the play she is a lively young woman, but in the trial scene she must pretend to be a sharp male lawyer. And third, she has to speak one of the most famous speeches in all the plays of Shakespeare: 'The quality of mercy …'

ELLEN TERRY

When Henry Irving played **Shylock** in the nineteenth century, the great actress Ellen Terry was Portia. A critic who saw her performance described it as

'gracious and graceful, handsome, witty, loving and wise … Portia to the life.'

Later in her life Ellen Terry spoke of Portia's famous speech as a moving and beautiful piece of poetry, but it is more than that. It comes at a crucial point in the trial scene where it first introduces the choice Shylock can make. He can go for full payment of the bond – his 'pound of flesh' – or compromise and show compassion. When Portia as the lawyer Balthasar praises the virtue of mercy, she is actually leading Shylock into a trap.

If he agrees with her, he loses face; if he disagrees and insists on repayment, she has a much greater shock ready for him – he can have Antonio's flesh, but not his blood.

Ellen Terry herself recognized this double-edged nature of the words. It is a magnificent and persuasive speech about a great human virtue. But Portia/Balthasar uses it to help the Christians trap Shylock and defeat him. Beauty is a bait, like jam to catch a fly. Throughout this interpretation, the idea was beginning to take hold that Portia was less morally perfect than we might think.

PEGGY ASHCROFT

When Peggy Ashcroft was first asked to play Portia in the 1930s, she was determined that she would approach the speech as 'a way of advancing the argument', not as a self-contained bit of poetry. A critic at the time commented that 'the speech arrived so suddenly I couldn't believe we'd got there'. Although the production as a whole (directed by John Gielgud) was criticized for its oddities, there is no doubt that Peggy Ashcroft's Portia, all 'innocence and humour', a young woman learning about love, has influenced many actresses who have approached the part since.

DEBORAH FINDLAY

If Ellen Terry noticed that Portia does not always behave as well as we might think a beautiful young woman should, then Deborah Findlay, in Bill Alexander's 1987 RSC production, was encouraged to explore these nastier parts of Portia to the full.

Venice here was a city full of racial hatred. Belmont was not a place of peace and beauty, but as one critic said, 'a place of creeping violence' and Portia on her home territory was vulgar – she had to be to control the loutish behaviour of **Bassanio**, **Graziano** and **Lorenzo**, but she seemed to get a kick out of it too. Her racist comments about the **Prince of Morocco** (so often cut) were left in. She seemed to hate Shylock quite as much as the men did. At least one critic was persuaded that this Portia was:

> '*... a stuck-up daddy's girl as nasty as she ought to be but so rarely is ...*'

Portia (Peggy Ashcroft) confronts Shylock (Michael Redgrave) in a 1953 production at Stratford.

PENNY DOWNIE

Deborah Findlay showed the unacceptable side of Portia. When Penny Downie began to prepare for the role in David Thacker's 1993 production, she and the director decided that Portia herself should embody 'the quality of mercy' and that Belmont should be as different as possible from Venice.

Penny Downie's picture of Belmont was as 'a spiritual place', 'a place of liberation and healing'. The racist comments were cut out of the text and Portia and **Nerissa** wore long flowing evening dresses which were a great contrast to the steel set and sharp suits of Venice.

Portia (Deborah Findlay) and Nerissa (Pippa Guard) at Belmont. Stratford, 1987.

FRIENDSHIP
AND FOOLING

Shakespeare's plays are full of friendships, deep relationships between two people who are often of the same sex, which give comfort and support, and often act as the springboard for change in characters' understanding of themselves. Rosalind and Celia, for example, in *As You Like It*, who run away together to the Forest of Arden; or Antonio in *Twelfth Night* risking death for his friend Sebastian in the midst of the confusions and madness of Illyria.

ANTONIO AND BASSANIO

Some interpretations of *The Merchant of Venice* have explored the complex friendship between **Bassanio** and **Antonio** in new and challenging ways. Is Bassanio pursuing **Portia** for her money? He's an extravagant man, who's borrowed from Antonio before. And what about Antonio? Why is he sad at the beginning of the play? Recent productions, especially Bill Alexander's at Stratford in 1987, have raised the possibility that Antonio is homosexual, frustrated in his love for Bassanio, and saddened by Bassanio's pursuit of Portia. He agrees to help Bassanio borrow from **Shylock** out of love, which is never returned.

LAUNCELOT GOBBO

The comic roles in Shakespeare's plays are of two main kinds: the clown and the fool. The fool tends to be sharp witted, a good singer with an important part to play in the way the plot develops – like Feste in *Twelfth Night* or the Fool in *King Lear*. Fools were like court jesters: entertainers who are allowed to speak the truth, however uncomfortable that might be. Clowns got their laughs by seeming less intelligent. They were often dressed as men from the country, outwitted by quick-thinking townsmen. The scenes in which these clowns appear are often simply opportunities for set-piece routines, like modern-day stand-up comics.

Christopher Luscombe as Launcelot Gobbo.
Stratford, 1993.

In many ways **Launcelot Gobbo** is a clown, not a fool. He has a long speech in which he wrestles with his conscience (should be leave Shylock or not?) which seems to be there not least to give an actor a comic routine. He has a scene with his father which appears to be little more than a chance for knock-about comedy, and maybe ad-libbing – making up lines on the spot, a hallmark of comedians throughout the centuries. (When Rob Edwards played Launcelot in 1981 he livened up his blind father's slow exit at one performance by telling him to 'Mind the canals'. The audience fell about laughing; the director was rather less pleased!)

Antonio (Clifford Rose) and Bassanio (Owen Teale) in the RSC production of 1993–94.

Christopher Luscombe, who played Launcelot at Stratford in 1993, discovered there is more to the part than mere clowning. Like a fool (such as Feste, or Touchstone in *As You Like It*), he gets drawn into the plot by acting as a go-between for **Lorenzo** and **Jessica**. His witty conversation with Jessica about becoming a Christian brings a new moral dimension to the play. For Luscombe, Launcelot Gobbo became a complex character: resentful of his father, fond of Jessica, jealous of Lorenzo. He was a clown, telling jokes, sharing his confusions with the audience; but he was a person too who went on an 'emotional journey … from oppressed Venetian servant to salvation at Belmont'.

THE MERCHANT OF VENICE
TODAY

In March 1996 in Konstanz, a town on the border of Germany and Switzerland, a group of young people – French and German speakers studying Shakespeare – performed in the English Bookshop extracts from several of the plays. Suddenly a young man pulled a skull cap from his pocket and put it on his head. He looked at the audience: 'Ich bin Jude,' he said. 'I am a Jew … If you tickle us do we not laugh? If you poison us do we not die?'

THE SHADOW OF ANTI-SEMITISM

Since 1945 all productions of *The Merchant of Venice* have had to face up to the horror of the murder of millions of Jews by the Nazis during the Second World War. Some people have thought that the play is so anti-Semitic that it should never again be performed.

Some have tried to show that it is much more sympathetic to **Shylock**, while others have explored the hatred of the Jews as a fact of European life which must be challenged and defeated within this very play. But no director, actor or member of an audience at *The Merchant of Venice* can now escape the long shadow of the Nazi concentration camps.

Of course many things happen in the play which are not directly connected to the question of Shylock's rejection, revenge and destruction. After all, Shakespeare's own company called it *The Merchant of Venice*, and it deals with questions of money and trade, trust and the law – all as vital in sixteenth-century London (or Venice or even Stratford, where Shakespeare's own father was a merchant!) as they are today.

'A pound of flesh': Shylock (David Calder) prepares to take what he is owed from Antonio (Clifford Rose). Stratford, 1993.

For David Thacker the situation went deeper. Shakespeare contrasts Venice, the place of money, the place where Shylock wants his 'pound of flesh', and Belmont, a place of 'generosity, compassion, love and kindness', as Thacker put it. His vision was that those qualities could spread to Venice, and even to the traders of Venice such as **Antonio** and **Bassanio**, making it a better place.

THE OUTSIDER

That was Shylock's vision too, in Thacker's production, but the Jew was trapped by intolerance and hatred until his hopes for co-existence – and even friendship – were changed into the one thought of revenge.

Wherever we look in the play, the uncomfortable questions about Shylock's treatment cannot be avoided. It always comes back to the Jew being the outsider. Even if, as Antony Sher played Shylock, he is flamboyant, shouting out loud his difference from the rest of the world, the question is raised: 'What made him like this?' Antony Sher's Shylock had a yellow Star of David sewn on to his gown. This production too had a prominent Star of David painted on the back wall like some Nazi graffiti. No one in the audience could forget the history which connected Shylock of Venice with the millions of Jews transported to camps, shot, burnt, poisoned:

'If you poison us, do we not die?'

What made the young man in Konstanz in 1996 want to play Shylock, want to speak that particular speech? The audience was aware first of how Shylock is no different from anyone else: Jew or Christian, all share a common humanity. But it became clear that if we make someone or some group second-class, then tolerance is twisted into hatred and friendship into revenge. Shylock shows just how hard tolerance can be.

'I am a Jew ...' David Calder's Shylock. Stratford, 1993.

INDEX